How to Write a Book
(In 48 hours)

Rich A. Lang

CONTENTS

INTRODUCTION

This is a project that came about due to a lot of time on my hands. I am quarantined to my home for the most part due to the COVID-19 virus of 2020 that really started in March of that year.

I was given the challenge to write a book in 48 hours without typing a single word by a friend.

Now under the rules, I can write the introduction and layout the guidelines. However, once I start the actual content, I can spend no more than 48 hours (not including final editing).

The only content excluded was the table of contents, links, and charts or graphics since I cannot dictate those items with any kind of accuracy. You already guessed it most likely I will speak the entire book without typing any of it – sort of. I will explain later as I cut through the bull as they say for those who make claims of this sort – yes I will also bring a dose of reality to the whole concept of "speaking a book" into existence.

Right now, I expect to cut and paste graphics for obvious reasons, but the goal is to dictate the majority of the book. I will give you the steps I used as you read through the book. I will also include options for using your phone to create a book without using expensive software.

1 INSPIRATION VS PERSPIRATION

There are books I have seen that say create a book in 30 days or some predetermined period of time, but I have not found any real earth-shattering advice that is any different from what I uncovered as I took this challenge.

I mean, choosing your topic is pretty straight forward I have a formula I follow (more on that later). I have published five books, but one I revised to make it more relevant. That is a fancy way of saying I polished up the content and made the final revision fit the vision I intended all along. I came across some very good research after publishing, and therefore, I removed the original version. I see many authors with 20 books and a lot are repeats with additional content to get their book count up. Sometimes it's hard to tell which one to buy given close release dates. I recently found an author I liked, so I downloaded 5 of his books through the Audible service to listen to. I was planning to attend a conference he was giving and I wanted to understand his ideas and position. By the way, he is a professional speaker contracted for engagements which explains some of the books. Having a new book is a great way to book the next engagement. However, after I read the third one, I had heard the personal stories multiple times repeated in more than one book. They were great stories, but there was a point where the content was diminished by repeating the same stories. I did not listen to the last two books. The writer had established his style. He would add content by referring to content from his previous works. For a new reader who read any one book, you would have likely said it was a well-written book with very moving stories. However, on this day, with technology, I downloaded 5 of his books. I had the unique ability to compare multiple books in a short while as I "serial read" three in a row consecutively.

 It's a shame because he is a very talented writer and is wonderful in person, however, I buy books to be exposed to new things and I was expecting the content that expanded on the previous ideas.

This is why I recommend you research unique topics then create your book with real honest research. Unique content will get you better reviews that are more consistent. Plus as a reader, you just enjoy fresh content more. It's just plain stimulating because it is new whether you agree or not. Thought-provoking content is suitable to stir up a good conversation, especially when it makes you hungry for more.

I also recommend you look at the reviews for books within your topic. Discover what readers are saying that is lacking with the book. Don't focus on a 5-star rating. You know those will be a glowing review and not likely teach you much you can use. Start with the ones with one star and find out what the reader did not like. This is how I built out additional content for this book. I saw several reviews that mentioned no links were provided for the resources the author was referencing about researching content. I wanted to provide a book that was more a tactical guide to the process. Publishing a book is more than just typing words. There is a process, and I wanted to go beyond how to write but include the mechanics of the process. I took that a step further and included the links I use plus a lot more for publishing, ghostwriters, transcribers, etc. I wanted to write a book that would sit near someone's desk with references they could use.

2 - WHAT DEFINES A (GOOD) BOOK

Let's start with size. Let me say millage will vary as they say. For every standard size, there is a contradiction.
My first book, " The Small Business Owners Guide," was 254 pages, 12 pt. font, single-spaced. I received my first royalty check from this book which I still have. I never cashed (yea, they were paper, not deposited to a PayPal account then). Don't be too impressed. It was very small. The check was just a symbol of my accomplishment and it meant I was not just a writer, but I had been paid for my work. I did not just write a book, but I sold many copies the first week, which was exciting. I still get an occasional royalty from that book throughout the year.

My second book, "Start a Career as a Top Sales Engineer," was 120 pages, 12 pt. font, single-spaced. It was largely based on a study of people in a profession that are the top 10% of wage earners. What habits differed from the other 80%-90% in the same field and how they formulated their work habits. I interviewed people to understand how they did their job and what was repeatable.

This is just a reference guide to give you some perspective of word count to pages in a book as an estimate.

Single-spaced 12pt font.
- 20,000 to 25,000 words = 100 page book
- 30,000 to 42,500 words = 150 page book
- 40,000 words = 200 page book.

Typical content based on subject:
- Short Stories 5,000 – 10,000
- Children's Book 500-600
- Middle School 20,000 – 50,000
- Novel 40,000

- Adult Fiction 80,000 – 100,000
- Romance 50,000

3 TRANSCRIBE OR NOT

This chapter is dedicated to cover different techniques and how to apply them. For example, I rely on Dragon Naturally Speaking for 90% of what I do. But it's not like I just sit down and talk. Sometimes I enjoy typing out some pages in MS Word when I have an idea I need to capture. I plan by creating an outline; then I do research to create notes about what I want to include. I have a lot of written notes or highlights in my outline down before I dictate to help me flow the idea.   There are many book ideas, but I can tell you the better books that get great reviews are those that the writer spent time researching and getting more details than just what you will find on the internet.   On average, a best-seller likely included a year of research for comparison. Doing a book in a short while can certainly be done and might be on a topic you know intimately from your profession. Remember if you are an expert on some subject, most of the world is not. Therefore you have an advantage already. There are also techniques beyond just using Google, yea there are other search engines and content engines to use. I will cover some of those later on and in the links section.

The goal here is to compare a higher-end solution and one that is a much lower cost for those on a tighter budget. I know not everyone can afford to run out and buy Dragon Naturally Speaking , which is in the $300 range for the latest version. I do want to give you some caution about Dragon. You can get version v13 for $69 on Amazon and other sites. The accuracy is not as good and requires more training. I purchased the latest version which was v15.3. It cost $360 + the headset with a boom microphone. At the time, the home version v15 was $119.00. You have to decide if it is worth it. There are minor differences between versions, such as the home edition does not allow you to create commands and supports one user. Not a big deal, but I decided I wanted no restrictions and it is a source of income so I bought the most expensive version. I think I could have gotten by on the $119 version just fine now looking back. I believe it is well worth the cost to get the latest version either way. I also did not consider upgrading my equipment until after I published several books so I am committed to writing more books. I invested in more expensive equipment to make this process easier. I don't suggest you do that until you know you like it or the technique works for you. You have to speak differently to "speak" a book. I will go into more of that later. I know plenty of people who published one book because it was an item on their "bucket list," as they say. The goal was complete and they will likely not publish another book. As I said, this is an additional income source for me, so I want to get better and improve my writing. I have taken courses and upgraded my equipment along the way. Publishing a book used to be a big deal, but with the digital options and self-publishing within everyone's grasp, we need to focus on quality and do the research to separate our work from those who just want to say they published a book.

I want to address speaking your entire book using a transcription service for someone writing their first book. There are some books that address the questions, but they are mostly based on their opinion, not any real evidence. When you first get introduced to the concept, it seems like magic. You likely thought what I did, this could be great. I just record some audio on my phone of me talking. Then send the files to a translation service and bingo I am a writer. We will find out just how realistic this is. I have tested both ways and include the results of my testing in this book.

The reason I even tried this challenge is I saw presentations from two people with the same idea but very different approaches. For both, I looked to see how many books they had published. For the first one, he had one book when I stated this project, and now has three. The second was a very seasoned internet marketer and I counted over 25 books on the first three search pages on Amazon (I believe he has over 100 total). I can easily say at first glance one might have a bit more credibility – however, not the case once you look closer.

You have to look at the quality of the writing and content. Some very successful full-time writers could retire after their first book, JK Rowling, who wrote Harry Potter as an example. Now, as I looked closer, I noticed the author with the most books was publishing a lot of 20-30-page books, which I call booklets, not books. If you can break a book into a course with 20 booklets and sell online, more power to you. The first one I looked at had 200-300 page books with a lot of research and good solid content. Understand the difference both have published books, but one was going for volume over quality content. The quantity technique was being used to get search ranking and drive traffic to his online training. The problem was the contact was weak; therefore, yes driving traffic, but short-lived. Define your goals. Do you just want something published or do you want to publish a book that people might discuss at the next book club.

Before we get too far ahead of ourselves, let's discuss techniques to get content transcribed to fit the definition of a book. I tested several transcription services for both accuracy and convenience. The problem is creativity does not always come when we want. Sometimes you get a great idea and need to be able to put down some notes in real-time. I like to create an outline of sorts. The outline would contain topic ideas that may be chapter names. The idea is to capture points I may want to research or find angles no one has covered about a particular topic or idea.

Tip: If you speak a book, put the information on PowerPoint slides. Then you can stay organized and won't miss anything. Then you can just do a presentation.

The comparison was made by using the same paragraph from one of the previous books I published. I would read it aloud to each service I tested. If they had a phone app I could use, I did. Again, convenience was more important to allow me to write or transcribe anywhere. I also used upload services where I used the audio app on my phone then upload the file to the service I was testing.

Sample Dictation:
To compare a pay for transcription service to a higher-end software dictation system, I used three pages from my "Small Business Owners Guide" book published in 2017. I read technique **#57 Get Testimonials** to test multiple options.
(The actual text read is at the end of this section)

For all the services I tested, I chose similar delivery and conversion options when possible. For example, for delivery, I decided next day when offered and Automatic conversion if available. A manual option means a person will sit and listen to the audio and type it out - this does cost more but is generally more accurate. This only holds true when the person translating is native to the language you are getting your transcript in, important to know. If not stated, ask before you use the service. It can be the difference in 99% and 90%. You don't want to edit a 90% conversion; it will have too many errors. Be careful when you see a low cost. Send one chapter or a few pages for a test. Different people within the same service will yield different results. You may articulate your words very well and an Auto conversion service works well enough as an example, or you need a manual service.

Be careful to be in a quiet room with no noise when you record if possible. This may allow you to use an Auto service, saving you a lot of money. Most important, don't speak like you are having a conversation. It will make it harder to translate. I found the best results using external services by pausing at the end of sentences and speaking slower than normal to articulate words better, especially names. This will help make the editing process go much smoother. If you have an accent in your speaking, slow your speaking down. I cannot emphasize this enough. If English is not your first language, then slow down and speak uncomfortably slow if your translator is native to English. I say uncomfortable because it will sound somewhat normal for the transcriber, just uncomfortable to you. I have noticed this with people from India who have an excellent English vocabulary but speak fast, not giving time for vowels to resonate. Therefore, the accuracy can go down. This is why you want to understand the native language of the translation service. If your translator has the same native language as you do but is translating into another language, your success is likely much higher. The person translating will be familiar with how you pronounce vowels, etc. We tested this and found much higher conversion results from the same translator when matching the native language, not the translated language.

My sample file was created from a Samsung S8 phone using the built-in voice recorder. After recording my voice, I used the same file for all testing so the baseline would consistent across all transcription services.

1) Rev.com ($1.25 per minute, 99% accuracy)
I uploaded it to the Rev.com website (all from my phone) 307 words for the test cost me $3.75 with a guarantee of a 48-hour turnaround.

One thing I do like about Rev is they offer a phone app that you can use to record live and convert, saving a couple of steps. The audio recorder is free. You pay when you select convert, which uploads the audio file. Some nice features like backing up data to Dropbox or working with Slack and Evernote to name a few. To convert each chapter as you speak it during your research, you could string your book out as you get the funds building chapter by chapter. Rev.com was by far the most user-friendly service I used.
Score: 100% accuracy

2) Scribe.com (.10 per minute Auto, .80 per minute Manual)

307 words, 2.43 minutes cost $1.00 for Auto version of service. Offered a great way to upload my audio and pay online. The whole process was quick and automated. However, the least accurate service I tried. They do offer a manual service at a slightly higher .80/min. rate, which I would recommend given the error rate on the automatic service. It's not worth saving .70 cents a minute if you have to spend a lot of time correcting simple errors. There may be additional charges for background noise and other parameters that could affect the translation.

There were 15 total errors in the document, 1 misspelled word, 6 punctuation, 8 grammar errors.

Fully automated – No human interaction

Score: 93% (+/- 5%) rated by Scribe – actual rate is 95% correct.
For only 307 words, that's a lot of corrections. Think of that as a third or less of a page depending on paragraph layout. That would be about 45 errors per page x 100 pages – not usable by any means.

Note: This is only for the Auto service, which works better for some other content types. The manual service is very accurate and worth the money.

3) GMR Transcription ($1.25 per minute) Charge for 24hr turnaround $3.70 per minute

307 words, 2.43 minutes cost $9.00 for the standard version of service, which is manual, no automation. They also have increased fees based on the delivery time chosen. Although they offer a $1.25 per minute fee, I would have to wait almost 14 days to receive my converted text.

They appear to offer more extensive translation services if you intend to offer your book in different languages. I will note the service is not as user-friendly as the other services I looked at. It did require extra steps, and the fees were not clearly explained. The $1.25 per minute fee advertised was a bit elusive, not clearly indicated on how to get that rate. I had to choose every delivery option to see the final cost. The advertised rate was clearly hidden from view and I spent some time before I located that option for that rate.

Most expensive option I tested
Manual Service – human typed translation
Score: 100% with correct punctuation

4) Attempt: Dragon Naturally Speaking

Please note the version matters. Dragon Naturally Speaking has improved the accuracy a great deal with newer versions. More emphasis is given to training on older versions. In the newer version, I did the training in a similar way but much less. I just did one exercise that took a few minutes. The results were very accurate. Now the way I spoke the test was different from the transcription services I evaluated. I spoke a sentence and said, "period" or "Comma" at the end. This allows Dragon to apply punctuation accurately since it recognizes that in the audio in real-time.

Now to be fair, I did not use this same technique with the transcription services. This was because the idea I wanted the ready to understand is how close you can get to a true transcription process with a natural conversation. My initial thought was, what if you found someone who was an expert in the topic you are writing about and recorded the audio just using the audio recorder on your phone. Well, the result is that it is a very realistic goal. Then you know you have quoted the expert correctly and can cut and pasted the output into your manuscript as needed.

For Dragon Naturally Speaking v15.3, no complaints; it did the job.
Score: 100% accuracy

Text used for all conversion services and techniques tested:
Technique #57

     It's been said before that one unsatisfied customer will go out and tell 20-50 of their friends and family about their unsatisfactory experience, but the opposite doesn't seem to occur. Your customers, vendors, suppliers and associates might think you walk on water, but they won't seem to tell everyone else how great you are unless you show them how and give them an actual reason to do it.

You can actually hold contests for best testimonials request letters of endorsement from your customers, vendors, suppliers, and any associates you have. Use those to promote your products and services. When you use testimonials to add credibility to what you do, you're letting your customers do the marketing for your business.

Testimonials from your customers are one of the strongest marketing tools available.

What is a testimonial? It's a statement, usually written by your customer, saying nice things about one aspect of your business, you, your employees, are your products and services. To use the testimonials in marketing efforts, you need to get a written release from your customers who wrote the testimonial giving your business the right to use the testimonial in marketing.

The best time to obtain the releases at the time the customer delivers the testimonial to you. You might tell them you want to share their insights with your customers or some other complementary statement.

When you use these testimonials, you want to weave them into your marketing story. Use them to embellish and support your claims and promises. For every benefit or objection, you need to overcome in your products or services. It is the best scenario to have testimonials establishing or referencing each benefit or objections.
You can take the next logical step and establish that your business delivers what it promises. This becomes a powerful statement.

Final thought on the transcription process.
Speaking in a natural conversation style while using your outline to guide you, use an Audio to Text conversion service, which can

be more comfortable   Just break the audio down in smaller "chunks" so you can check the quality easier.

I use three folders when organizing a book:
1 – Audio (Original audio recordings)
2 – Converted Audio (File from conversion service)
3 – QA Proofed (Final Text I have proofread)

For a dictation product like Dragon Naturally Speaking, you must speak punctuation. It takes getting used to and not so naturally speaking, no pun intended. You have to say "Period" at the end of a sentence, or "Period", etc. when you want to add punctuation. You can do some corrections like "Bold" a word, but that takes more time and knowledge. However, it can take more time to proofread your converted files from a service and insert punctuation as well. This is something to also look out for. Some conversion services consider the conversion done once all words are typed. This is why a manual service can be good if they are native to your language. A native speaker will type and add some punctuation naturally as they type. Periods are added when they hear a pause but may miss a lot of commas, so don't expect to get a perfect conversion. Regardless of the method you choose, there is still some work involved to get to the final edit stage before you are ready to publish. You can also remember to speak in complete sentences as much as possible and avoid the need for semi-colons or commas to speed up the process. Not suggested you sacrifice your writing style or quality, just pointing out what takes time over efficiency.

Also, as an additional option, you can find many options on **Fiverr.com**. You will find an average cost of $5 for 15 minutes of audio. However, most of these offers will be foreign or have English as a second language. Although you can filter sellers by your native country. You have to look at the seller's bio or profile information to find country or origin. I did not list any specific seller links because my experiences were varied. When I used someone not native to the US, the English was what we would call proper English, missing adjectives sometimes as they had a more difficult time with English Slang. There are some excellent quality services on Fiverr, but you may have to look and even try a few to find one you can rely on. For some it's just extra money, for others, it is their full-time job so the attitude is very different and so is the quality. US-based translators will typically also cost more.

However, the cost does matter during the creation since you cannot sell what you have not written. If you are a well-established writer, you can pre-sale a book before you create it, but that takes time and good quality writing usually or just a lot of creativity. The bigger issue is you need to be very organized and have a process that works to do this. For example, do you have a research process that would allow you to expand on a topic quickly? Do you just need time to write? Can you dedicate time each day to write and not miss a day until the book is completed? Here is the big question to ask yourself; if contracted to write a 200-page book, accurately estimate how long it will take. If you have not written a book before or maybe just one, then it may be hard. You need a structured template to track and organize your book project. If the book is 200 pages and you want to publish it in 90 days, you need to write about 2.5 pages per day. That includes weekends and holidays. Planning is essential, don't just jot notes down for two months, then think you can easily put them together into a book. I tried; it's tough to be that un-organized and meet a deadline. I sometimes have a folder for each chapter, so my notes are well organized for that part. I have been traveling, and while at lunch, something provoked a creative spark, so I jotted the idea down on a napkin. When I got home, I dropped the note into the folder for that chapter until I was ready to work on it.

Cost may not be a big issue for 307 words, however, to put that into perspective, let's look at a 150-page book. The average 150-

page book has about 30,000 words.

30,000/307 = 97.71 audio recording files to complete a 150-page book.
Based on the charges from the above testing of the different services.

- $9 per 307 words spoken = $879
- $3.75 per 307 words spoken = $362
- $1 per 307 words spoken = $97
- .10 cents per 307 words spoken = $30.70
  (Note: @ .10 cents per word the error rate is high)

Speaking a book into a published manuscript is somewhat a myth. Everything here is a tool used correctly. It can save you a lot of time and allow you to find a method that works well for you. I spent a year on one book. I almost gave up several times. I then developed a process with templates that work for my style. I have preformatted book templates for Microsoft Word in the 6x9 standard book format. This means I can paste the text into it and submit it when ready to publish. If you search for books on Amazon, look at the book page count and read the reviews. You will notice a smaller 20-30-page book better be really good with mostly quality content that is very focused, or it gets negative reviews since there is little room for fluff. In a larger 200-300-page book, you will find more research to validate ideas and support the author's viewpoint.

We don't need more books; we need more quality manuscripts with information to expand our knowledge.

4 LET THE RESEARCH BEGIN

You need to make sure there is a market for your book.
Take 1 hour to research and create a top 10 list.
Then narrow that down to your final project based on two
main criteria.

1) You see a lot of general interest, meaning the topic is on
multiple sources (social media, news sites, books being sold,
hobbies, etc.)

2) You have verified that the topic is not overdone or has a
unique twist to a common topic.

For example, how many books on your topic are on Amazon.
If there are 500, it may be difficult to get yours noticed if you
self-publish.

I look for topics that interest me and then look to see what is
available and what is trending.
For trending look at Facebook, you can find a group to join for
just about anything out there you can image. Just read a post
occasionally and see what people are talking about.

Ask my favorite question, "What is the most significant issue
with _____ in this group?"
Second favorite question, what solutions have been suggested
so far? It's not just about what matters but has anyone
actually done anything or is this just a place for a voice to
complain. Now you may be on to something; do the research
find out what options are available.

Reddit - https://www.reddit.com/ can provide content on what
people are interested in. Look for a subreddit to watch and
gather data.

Quara - https://www.quora.com/ this is a great place to post a question to get some input. You can comment on some else's question and see how they respond or search on your topic to find data from experts. Ask a question to help with your research; you may get some great responses.

For Amazon specifically, there are browser plug-ins that can increase your visibility and awareness on products to sell or track (links provided in index):

Unicorn Smasher:
Developed by the makers of AMZ Tracker, **Unicorn Smasher** is a free Amazon product research tool that can help you find profitable products to sell on Amazon, to get to the whole purpose of your business on the platform.
(Link in index)

Amazon Assistant:
It is also available as an **Android** app. **Amazon Assistant** notifies you of shipments and deliveries. When you browse other websites, it will display similar products on **Amazon**, and ratings and reviews.

DS Amazon Quick View:
This allows you to quickly glance at important product information, such as product ASIN, sales ranking, customer rating, and more direct info on the Amazon index pages.

Look at the best sellers on Amazon to see what is selling.
From: http://www.amazon.com
 Search on Best Selling books
 You can also specify the year, etc.

On the left, you will see the categories or departments you can see what is ranking. Here is an example of one shown as the #1 ranked book. However, also notice it is only in specific categories, so the rating does not necessarily translate to revenue. It shows a comparison to other books in the same category.

Best Sellers in Books

You can also see sales data on how the book is priced. Look at books in a similar category to decide how to price yours. This book appears to have started around $28 for a short period, then lowered the price to $17.

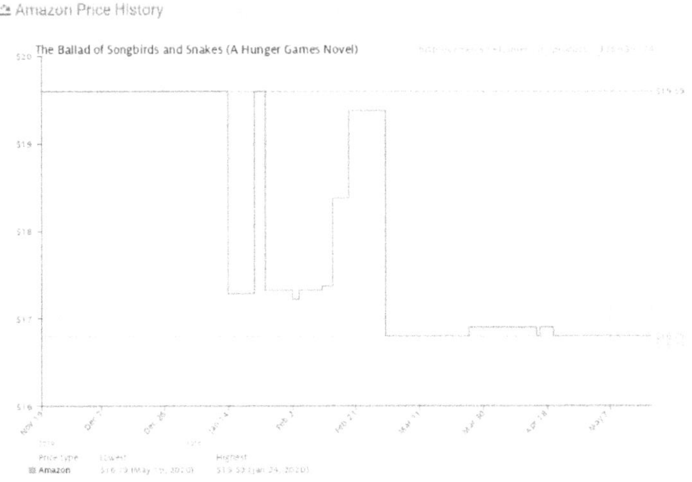

Currently, the book was selling for $16.79.

Amazon charges $0.15 per megabyte (MB)— for the file size of your Kindle eBook. There is no delivery fee for **books** priced below $2.99 or above $9.99. When trying to decide how to price your book, consider the average price between $2.99 and $9.99. One of the reasons for the low average is there are bookstores that sell books for .01 or .99 plus shipping for marketing reasons. I don't think this is a good idea because the likelihood this would create loyalty to get me to buy from them again is low. I will look for a book I want then check the price against all suppliers. Amazon has a perceived loyalty that comes from a better price, access to so many titles and free shipping to Amazon Prime members.

Now I am not advocating you sell your hard work for pennies on the dollar. Just the opposite, evaluate the value and ask yourself if you include enough value, unique points and how well do you do at convincing someone to take your perspective. Good copy has a value and yours might be worth a lot more. For example, a 375-page novel is reasonable to price at $16.95. You will find most come between $6.95 to $19.95. You need to research other books in your category to decide the best price. The price which is relative to the marketing behind it.

- Do you plan a marketing campaign before you launch the book?
- Are you going to get samples to ship to major book resellers?
- Do you have a publisher that is willing to work with you?

If you have a publisher, most will require you do not publish on any other platform. If you publish on Amazon, that may disqualify you from being published. A publisher wants to control every aspect, including the marketing and audience. If you are self-publishing, you might be more in line to charge $5.99 or less since you are relatively unknown, and maybe your topic is not as popular, so all things need to be considered. Some publishing houses will market your book for a fee. You can choose the marketing and set a budget. One thing that makes Amazon attractive is the ability to market your book when you publish. I typically take advantage of this. It's just too easy not to. Remember these are things you need to consider before you publish while the book is new and the content is fresh. The value of your marketing campaign will diminish once the book has been published, so think this through and plan ahead.

In the beginning, when you would create your book you could use Create Space to build the book. You would upload the content and the cover. Once this was done, you could go to the KDP marketplace at https://kdp.amazon.com/ to publish your book as a Kindle book and a paperback book. You could also order proof copies to see what your book will look like when others order a copy. Create Space is now part of the KDP market space.

5 - THE OUTLINE

Once you get your topic, you need to determine the questions that will eventually become your chapter names. For example, ask yourself what someone would like to know about the topic you have chosen. Using five or six questions could be the chapter names. For each chapter, you will explore the details and include your research to answer the question.

Let's use Woodworking as an example
To build an entertainment center, what should you consider someone needs to know before starting?

1) Where can you get plans
   Free and paid
2) Tools required and Optional
   Can you use only hand tools
3) Deciding on the features
   Draws, Glass Doors
   Lights
   Hidden Compartments
4) What type of wood is best
   Finished or Raw
   Pro and cons with raw wood that has to be planed
   Joinery: Glue, Dowels, Screws or Nails
5) Understanding finishes
   Should you consider water-based finishes
   Is polyurethane good enough
   Is spar varnish better
6) Building modular components with moving in mind
7) Sources for Tools, Electronics
8) What if I wanted to sell my product to furniture stores

9) Determining Pricing
10) Delivery options

Now I have laid out 10 potential questions to answer.
I may combine some chapters to increase content and page count within a single chapter. If you run out our questions, think about being at a conference and someone wants you to answer general questions. Then try to come up with the hardest question you can from an outsider viewpoint. Consider things slightly off-topic, after all, you are the supposed expert, so any question is fair game in front of the media. If this is difficult, then email yourself questions and reply with the answers. This sounds kind of off, but when you type, you come up with more content than if you just speak it at the moment. Thought is required allowing you to expand more.

Once you have broken down the chapter names, you are will on your way. You need to come up with what you will address in each chapter. Think about what a reader would want to know. For example, put yourself in their shoes for a minute. If I saw a chapter that said, "Understanding Finishes," as a reader, I can think of things I hope the chapter contains.

- Where is the best place to get stains?
- What about the stains at Home Depot or Lowes? Are they different?
- There are many brands. What do the professionals use?
- What if I mess up? How do I fix finish problems.

A new woodworker is likely intimidated and wants to know what to do if the inevitable happens. Is there a difference in products to use for personal use or if I am selling the product. I would not use affiliate links in a book, but in a digital copy, it might work. If you do, be very clear to own that you have included affiliate links. You have to be careful some people get turned off quickly when they find you are directing them to a way for you to get paid.

Ok now break each chapter down with again five or six questions to answer within this chapter. There are so many forums on furniture refinishing I should have no problem finding content and many links I use for my reference page as well.

Plus, watching a dozen videos on YouTube® then summarizing the finishing techniques you learn in this chapter. Think about that for a minute. You watch a few hours of YouTube, then consolidate that into a few paragraphs. That is a valuable use of any readers' time. It's all about how much usable content you can provide in a single manuscript.

6 BUILDING CONTENT

After I wrote my first manuscript, I gave it to someone to review. The response was, you've done a lot of research and the content is good, but not sure what to do with this. You did not lead me to take any action or draw any significant conclusion.

I learned a very important lesson. You cannot just present a lot of content. You have to tell the reader what they should expect. Then take them by the hand and lead them down the path. Present the information, then tell them in summary what you recommend and present the call to action. It does not matter if you are selling a product or selling your story. You must take the reader to the very end and not expect them to draw any conclusion on their own. They won't. They will leave disappointed and unsatisfied.

Also, don't expect a best seller out of the gate. A "best seller" takes a lot of research and good quality editing. A good best seller will take a lot of research. You will find a lot have a publishing house behind them. It is not that you can't do it by self-publishing. You just likely won't know all the tricks of the trade to speak with your first book.

The average person can type 38-40 words per minute. This means if you type at 40 words per minute, you should be able to finish a 150-page book in a little over 12 hours to put that in perspective. Not likely, why you might ask? Well, you won't type at 40 words per minute non-stop. You will occasionally stop to gather your thoughts or maybe even verify some light research you jotted down as relevant but have not looked into yet and somewhere in there, you will likely eat and sleep before the book is finished. This is the reason for a good outline. The better your outline, the more you can flow. I want a rough outline because as I review each thought, I will expand on it differently than I would have when I had the initial thought. Plus, when I leave to eat or whatever, I need to find where I left off quickly. I want my time to be used efficiently, not trying to determine where I left off each time when I sit down to write.

One thing you might consider is using index cards. List your questions on each card. Then expand how you would address the answer, where you would look for the answer and elaborate on the details. Jot down notes on each index card. Next thing you know, you have an outline for a new chapter. The question What Stains are available, becomes How to Choose the right stain. This could then go into durability, inside vs. outside stains and finishes. You could watch a dozen YouTube videos on this topic alone.

I can't caution you enough on not trying to be perfect. Strive to get data captured. You want a "loose" version initially to be sure your idea flows. If you spend too much time reading and rereading a chapter, you will find yourself with too many questions and question yourself. Get out of your head and just strive to base the idea on your outline flow captured. Follow the flow and chapter layout and you can organize later. The most important thing is consistency. Set time each day to work on it even if you can only spare 30 minutes – DO IT! If you let too much time pass between writing periods, it will slow you down. You will have to reread what you wrote previously to find your starting place. If you sit there and nothing comes to mind, fine, type in topics into Google and look for new results or search amazon to look for new published books on your topic. Just do not let too much time pass before reviewing your manuscript or you start to forget what you have covered. I had life happen and just wrote nothing for 2-3 months, then had a great thought of something to include only to find out I included some of the thoughts in a previous chapter. I also included major points in my outline so I could see I had included particular aspects. Not a perfect solution but helps me get back on track when I have not been able to write for a few days, weeks or months.

Your goal should be around six pages minimum per chapter. Try to create six chapters minimum to start. Now that is only 36 pages and a far cry from a book. The idea is to form the basic foundation and expand on each chapter. For example, when I wrote "Start a Career as a Top Sales Engineer," it was 120 pages with 21,486 words and contained 10 chapters. This also required a .25" spine I had to make sure the book cover accounted for so the title was centered correctly. A book cover designer on Fiverr did this for me (a link to Fiverr in the last section). Once I had the basic foundation, it was pretty easy to expand and even add several chapters later. I had chapters in the table of context but did not include page numbers. I added the page for each chapter at the end before publishing.

There are a few ways to write the book.
Type all the words – I think we all know what this means and in some cases, if you did not learn to type, this might mean two fingers typing and that takes time (you know who you are).

Transcribe using software – There are many options like Dragan Naturally Speaking as an example. Other options in the links section at the end. The concept is you wear a headset and speak the book while the software writes – not as simple as it sounds as I stated earlier. You have to train yourself to some extent to use this method.

You can transcribe audio then send to a transcription service and about the easiest you could ask for. This is an excellent step for a repeatable option. You speak the book as with software, but you don't buy the software. You can even use your phone to record the book. You send or upload the files to the transcription company and they send back the digital files nicely typed for a fee. This is one of the most cost-effective options for a new writer on a budget.

Use a Ghostwriter
This is a very lucrative option. There are two ways this can work. You can give a partial manuscript or your outline to the Ghostwriter or you can provide them with a topic and how many words you want to purchase. This has become much more affordable than it was a few years ago. Maybe just more people are doing it. I am not sure. However, I looked several years ago and it was pretty expensive. I would guess just more people offering the service has contributed to a lower price. I have seen a 300-page book vary from about $900 to $5,000 or more. For the $5,000 option, the writer told me not to provide any data, only provide the topic and any details I wanted the book to include. He had a few celebrities on his list of accomplishments. He was producing good quality, but at a cost, not many will absorb. Yes, the quality also varies widely with this service. Some Ghostwriters had a menu of options or additional charges to add photos, and verify original content, copyrights, etc. You get the idea; you need to also decide how sellable your book really is.

What is the market? Do you have potential buyers lined up? I know writers who create the content in outline form and have someone design a great cover. Then they pre-sale the book. If they make enough from the pre-sale, they hire a ghostwriter and go on vacation. Few of us have that kind of fan base or disposable cash. Well, you have to start somewhere, and that is not a bad goal to have. Harry Potter was not popular until it was. What I mean is out of the gate, it had to grow a fan base. Look at the later releases where people would stand in line at midnight to get the first copies. Kind of insane, but that is a loyal fan base in action. I interviewed one writer who said they research many book ideas a lot don't make it.   I think that is very typical; I have had ideas I thought were great, then saw many books on the subject and decided the topic was a bit overdone.   With this book, I researched the topic and found several books to review. All of the ones I looked at were repeating similar information and missed a lot on the topic like the truth about what works and what does not.   Most books focused on technique, not on the logistics of how to do it and gather material or one of the most important steps for research.

Depending on what you choose, you are likely to need an editor.

The editor's function is to review your manuscript for errors and grammar mistakes, including misspelled words. A good place to find an editor is on Fiverr, which can offer many services from individuals. Like a cover designer, and editors. My personal experience is making sure you are happy with the work before you accept anything. I hired a cover designer who did a good job. I accepted the work because it looked great.   Then I discovered the cover was not the correct size and the publisher rejected the work. I had to spend a few hours cutting and pasting to reformat until it passed submission requirements.   I only had this experience once, so just be aware of making sure everything is correct before accepting.   Fiverr allows you to keep asking for revisions. If you don't, your job will auto-accept. In my case, the person I was working with said I accepted his work, so basically, have a nice day. For the editor, they did a superb job and I made no further edits.   They also offered to expand my chapters if I wanted a larger book. I did ask for expanding the book. The editor estimated it would be about 100 pages and wanted an additional $800. I decided not to and was glad I did. Here it seemed like it would include information that was not my idea. This book was about my experiences and impact from a particular industry. Therefore I decided not to expand, but it was nice to know that option did exist. If you did not finish a chapter, you could have the editor do the research and add it for you.

7 - DO'S AND DON'T'S

You want to be careful about making your book too long. I know most first-time writers are more worried about having enough content. I recently reviewed a book with 300 pages in 9 pt. font. It was hard to read and included 14 chapters. I felt like it would take forever to get through. I was interested, but I wondered why the author did that. If it was 10 or 12 pt. font, it would have been double the amount of material. I would have made two books, given the amount of valuable content. This could easily be a three-volume set, each released six months apart to gain readers along the way. Even better, this could be a short manuscript and lend to online training for additional revenue possibilities. You get the idea. Always be thinking about how to expand your option. The book should advertise your online training course. This guy focused on putting everything possible in one book. Thank you, done.   I never finished the book. I eventually lost interest in wading through the material to get to a few great nuggets of value.

You will want to proofread your book to be sure the flow is correct. Make sure it flows, your grammar is correct, and there are no misspelled words. Now don't spend too much time. I would not expect to catch everything. This is a high-level run-through to be sure you captured your thoughts the way you wanted to. Spend no more than 30 minutes per chapter. You are not rewriting, just checking to make sure you captured the thought the way you initially intended.

I have read a book many times, then had someone else read it and found a misspelled word in the first chapter. The problem is you are just too close to the material to catch everything.

This is the number one reason you want an editor. For a 150 page book, you are likely to pay around $1 a page or more for a good editor. Several sites specialize in editing and other services but may cost you more. I found a good editor on Fiverr who did the work in about four days and did a great job catching many issues I missed before publishing including some bad grammar. You can read a document many times and miss simple things. This is why it is very important to have a second set of eyes review before publishing.

An editor will typically charge by the word. Expect to pay around $32 for editing a 5,000 words manuscript. This will vary based on experience and rating. For an editor from the Fiverr.com site, a Level 1 editor would be about $130 for 11,000 words or about 50 pages of material. For a Pro+ certified writer, that same book would be $300. Only about 1% get the Pro+ certification. Now, why would I pay $300? Well, that comes with a lot more services. The Pro+ rating also will include structure and flow recommendations that go beyond just punctuation and bad grammar. If you are doing a novel, this may be necessary to help significantly improve the final product for readability. If you are publishing a how-to or DIY book, grammar and punctuation may be enough. For this book I used the $130 service.

8 Choosing your Title

I saved choosing the title last because I typically choose a title to work from in the beginning. However, it evolves a bit before the final page is completed. Some titles I choose withstand the process and become permanent. Others I have evolved several times.

Your title should be short and generally show the reader about the subject the book focuses on.

You want a more descriptive subtitle that tells the reader what area of the subject you will be focusing on with this book. The subtitle can help with search results to provide broader coverage.

As an example, if your book is about Sales, you might have a title of Increase Sales with a subtitle of For the Catering Industry, etc. This tells the reader it is sales-related but very specific to the catering market. Don't want car salesmen buying that book. They will likely give bad reviews. Now that allows the reader additional information to tell if it is worth looking further.

I don't want to ever mislead a potential reader. I want to honestly gain their interest and hopefully satisfy what they are looking for with a unique angle on the information. I am not trying to make every detail unique. However, I want to strive to have some new "nuggets" of information for every reader that pics up one of my books. That starts with a good, carefully chosen title.

For one book, I did a lot of marketing research on the top

books selling in my category. I also looked at top Google searches. I paid someone to do additional search term research I found on Fiverr. After this, I changed the title to include two of the top words searched on. When I published the book, I got some immediate sales I attribute to this tactic. I did this as an experiment to see how much it would affect my sales. I would not do this every time because sometimes a title can be very specific and needs to reflect the content in a particular way. Maybe you just have an emotional connection to the book and the title needs to reflect that. In my specific case, I was writing a DIY book, and therefore, it made perfect sense to gain an advantage from the search engines.

9 PUBLISHING OPTIONS

I am devoting a more extensive overview to Kindle Publishing because it is the one most people are gravitating to because it is easy. If you are like me and want to update or revise a book later, the KDP service is easy to do so. It is not the only one or even the best one; however, given the number of products Amazon sells, it makes sense to publish here for good exposure. That's the good news; the bad news is Amazon has so many books you have to distinguish yourself to get noticed. It's not as bad as it seems. Amazon will give you a score that determines where you show up in the ratings. Being a newly published book will give you points in the ratings to show up. The category can help as it is one of the top searches. A lot of things play into this. Below is an example of the KDP publishing screen. This is called the "bookshelf". From here, you can publish and make changes. For example, if your book has been published for over 90 days and it's not showing up in a general search, you can change the price of your book and republish. If you make a small edit, that is considered republishing. Remember, it could take 24 hours to be available since a republishing will require a review by Amazon before being live again. It cannot be purchased during this review period.

You can see below the book "Want to be an SE" has been removed from publishing and is no longer available to purchase. I would have to click "continue setup" to provide it again. The book above it, "Start a Career as a Top Sales Engineer," is a rewrite with a lot of new content, so I published the new manuscript and removed the original publishing. I considered a Volume II option but felt it was a better idea to publish the book that was complete with a new chapter and about 50 pages more content along with a new cover design.

Amazon Kindle Dashboard

https://kdp.amazon.com/en_US/

After logging in, you will see the following referred to as your bookshelf. This is after the manuscript has been uploaded along with the cover and approved. You can also advertise from here. I typically create a budget for my new book to advertise when I launch. I decide the amount and duration based on how popular the topic is among other things.

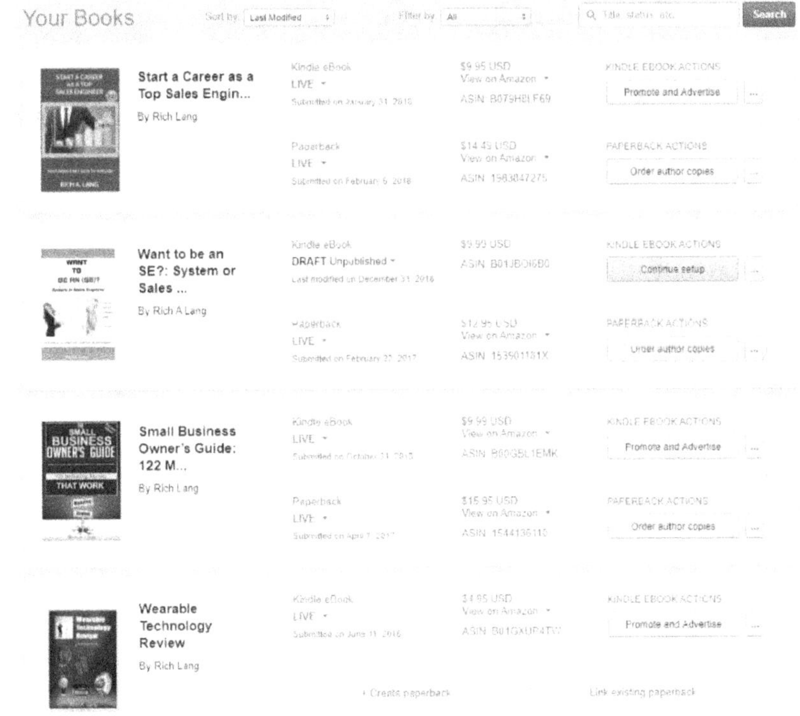

There are options on many sites where you can offer a course or manuscript for sale. They handle the payment for you. You could have a single-page website commonly referred to as a squeeze page, to redirect users to purchase your book or material.   The links on your website could be a redirect to Amazon, so you don't have to handle payment processing.

Let me frame this out a bit for you. You will find links in the index at the end for places you can host a free website. You could use Fiverr to hire a freelancer to build a single-page website for your book. You should expect to pay between $10 and $40. The page could have a link to Amazon to purchase the book. The free hosting sites do not charge you unless you use advanced services like ecommerce to collect payments. You could then spend time on blogs and forums to locate people that have a similar interest. Ask someone if they would mind reviewing your book. The purpose would be to post the link in that blog for others to see, provided they agree. Never just post the link without permission.

If they later provide a positive review, include it in the book or on the back cover. If you want a publishing house to publish for you, this is typically something they will push hard to get before publishing. In this book, I use the example of building some furniture. For example, I could go to YouTube and look for woodworkers with 100K views. Then ask several if they would review my book. My offer to them for a positive review would be free advertising. I would list the review on the back cover with a link to their website.

Other options to sell your book or manuscript that handle the payment for you are:

- **Rakuten Marketing**
- **CJ Affiliate Network**
- **Market Health**
- **Affiliate.com**
- **PeerFly**
- **GlobalWide Media**
- **ShareASale**
- **Amazon Associates Program**
- **eBay Partner Network**

The alternative is paying for a website and eCommerce fees to get a way for a customer to buy your book. Each site here does something different and attracts a different market. I did not list these at the end because I don't endorse any of them specifically. I have had both positive and negative experiences. You need to explore many options and build a market plan. Your plan should include both a budget and activity you plan. For example, if you publish on Kindle Publishing, the dashboard has advertising options for each book to make it easy. Plan for what you will do during the initial launch and 30 days out. What about a single page on a website that redirects people to a place to purchase like Amazon or one of the options listed above. Then search about google ranking and pick one as part of your launch plan to get that single web page to rank for the topic, title or subject. Now that may sound complicated or difficult depending on your experience and background. I know it's likely a lot for a first-time publisher. Leverage sites like Fiverr to find Google ranking experts. They will do the heavy lifting for you. My point here is to create a plan for success. What is the saying, "If you don't plan for success, you plan to fail" or something like that? It is so true. Don't haphazard expect a book to sell just because it is listed on Amazon and the Amazon link is in your signature of your personal emails. You will find your friends and family will congratulate you and even call you an author – so nice to hear. It's not likely any one of them will purchase your book. You might get some sympathy purchases, but let's be realistic here.

I know a lot of people who published a book and got great accolades for doing so. It was a major accomplishment for them. No real research or market studies. They just thought the world needed their book. A year later no sales, not even one. Never publish a book because you think the world needs it. Publish a book with the idea you want to convince the world of your argument or position.

Ok now you wrote your book for a market you researched before you started, right?

Ok, then the next step is research how to make your market aware you just released something they need. This is what they have been waiting for and now it's available at a discount for the book launch. It is your job to tell people they need your book. Never think you are presenting information; you are convincing people you are right.

10 CONCLUSION

- Set your goals high you can accomplish your first book by spending 20 minutes a day. Be diligent each day; you will find excitement grow. Leverage it to help finish the book and be proud of your accomplishments.
- Don't be discouraged by slow sales. Order copies for yourself to give away or leave in the doctor's office when you're in the waiting room. Some people will take a quick picture and order later. It's the times we live in.
- Depending on your topic, who would be interested? If it's a children's book think about civic centers or children's museums; always have one with you to drop and leave behind. I once had someone ask me to speak and we discussed my book. I got a job offer out of it. They did not care about the book as much as the fact I published it. He never read it but told everyone a published author was going to speak. I got paid and that was cool.
- Follow the formula for each book; don't go overkill. Remember, most books do better in the 100 – 200 page range with 6-8 chapters.
- There are enough sources to outsource every aspect of a book. You can even get a ghostwriter to write the entire book for a very reasonable amount if you choose.

Total Cost to Produce "How to write a book in 48hrs"
1. Book Cover Design   - $25
2. Copy Editing   - $130
3. Transcribing Research   - $13.75
4. Ad copy for Amazon listing - $35.00
5. Amazon Marketing   - $100.00

    Published Book   - $303.75

A lot of people want you to believe you can publish a book in 48 hours – yea, I realize it's the title of this book. It is possible, so I won't discount the idea altogether – I did build the content for this book in 48 hours, so it's a win. However, let me put things in perspective. Now let's say you get all the audio portion only for your book within 48 hours. We won't count the editing, cover design and publishing process, just the creation part you can control. Then you might have a weak manuscript unless you just get one of those ideas that explode out of you and lock yourself in a room for the weekend – maybe not likely and no, not what I did. The problem is how most people write in segments and don't mention anything about research. A good quality book can take a lot of time to research. A true bestseller takes work to write, edit and be ready to market. I can only speak from my own experiences. I begin to write and an idea or topic will unfold. I typically will do some research, then write that down and build a chapter. I will do this cycle so I can focus on each topic to keep the flow moving. Again let me emphasize a big problem for many writers is not spending time each day and you can forget what you included and have to read what you wrote again to make sure you don't repeat yourself.

For this book, I did the research beforehand to be sure I was comfortable with the flow. I laid out my thoughts in an outline in PowerPoint for the chapters. Then I spoke the content in less than 48 hours. I can tell you if you start telling, you are likely to start and restart a few times before you are comfortable. Take a lot of notes and organize them by chapter. You will also find once you know the topic well enough, you can talk freely for each chapter and the content will begin to flow. I only needed an outline just to keep me on track once I had completed my research.

After everything I have experimented with, I can tell you I will use Rev.com for audio to supplement my Dragon Naturally Speaking because sometimes while researching, it's just not convenient. I also travel a lot to speak a chapter into my phone using the app in my Hotel room. Rev was the only company that offered that option at the time. I will combine the different methods, including the old fashion typing method to get the most efficient use of my time. I found several services that were accurate, but each required more time investment to get great results. Interestingly the most expensive service was the hardest to use. It was difficult, but I had to click into the site more than any other service to upload my audio and retrieve the transcription. It was not very user-friendly.

The biggest suggestion I can offer is putting some words down every day and not getting too hung up on accuracy. Always carry a pad and pen with you. Sitting in a doctor's office waiting for a checkup, I got an idea for another chapter and jotted down an outline and some ideas. You just don't know what will trigger a new creative idea or thought. I have been in a waiting room and asked someone next to me a question I created from my list. I told them it was research for a project and explained I had to ask a stranger. They loved the idea and gave me great feedback about what details they would want the book to provide. Get content recorded in some way, then go back and do a rough edit later. Get something in print. Take the first step. The second always follows and is easier than the first.

11 LINKS | REFERENCES

- Content
- Publishing
- Editors
- Book Cover Design
- Advertising

Finding content to write about:
- https://ezinearticles.com/
- http://www.Amazon.com

Keyword tool for Google Chrome to find out what kind of information people are looking for:

Keywords Everywhere is a freemium chrome extension that shows you monthly search volume on 15+ websites.

It shows you "related" keywords as well as "people also search for" keywords.
https://chrome.google.com/webstore/detail/keywords-everywhere-keywo/hbapdpeemoojbophdfndmlgdhppljgmp

DS Amazon Quick View
Add amazon ranking and sellers information to the search page
https://chrome.google.com/webstore/detail/ds-amazon-quick-view/jkompbllimaoekaogchhkmkdogpkhojg

Unicorn Smasher: https://www.unicornsmasher.com/
Helium 10: https://www.helium10.com/

Get information to build your content:
www.yahoo.com/answers
www.dogpile.com
www.duckduckgo.com
http://www.infotopia.info/

https://books.google.com/

Sciences

https://www.wolframalpha.com/
https://worldwidescience.org/
https://www.science.gov/
https://eric.ed.gov/
https://www.researchgate.net/search

Education Academic Sites

https://www.refseek.com/
https://scholar.google.com/
http://www.virtuallrc.com/
https://education.iseek.com/iseek/home.page
https://academic.microsoft.com/home
https://scholar.google.com/
https://www.base-search.net/

Medical Healthcare

https://www.ncbi.nlm.nih.gov/pmc/

Legal Topics

https://signin.lexisnexis.com/lnaccess/app/signin?back=https%3A%2F%2Fadvance.lexis.com%3A443%2F&aci=la

Book Cover Design and Editors:

https://fiverrrus.fiverrpal.app/

Ghost Writing Service

https://ewritersolutions.com/product/ebook-writing/
https://ghostwritingsolution.com/
https://reedsy.com/ghostwriting/book-ghostwriter
https://gothamghostwriters.com/

Publishing Options

- Create Space
  https://www.createspace.com/

- Smash Words
  https://www.smashwords.com/about/how_to_publish_on_smashw
  ords?gclid=EAIaIQobChMItYjByOya6AIVmh-tBh1zuQ-
  eEAAYASAAEgLJLfD_BwE

- Publish Drive
  https://www.publishdrive.com/

- Draft 2 Digital
  https://www.draft2digital.com/

- Rakuten Kobo
  https://www.kobo.com/us/en/p/writinglife
- Google Play Books
  https://play.google.com/books/publish/

- Barnes and Nobles
  https://press.barnesandnoble.com/

Transcribing Services

Rev Services
- https://www.rev.com

Scribe Audio Transcription
- https://scribie.com/

GMR Transcription
- https://www.gmrtranscription.com

Transcribing Software
Dragan Naturally Speaking Software

- https://www.amazon.com/Nuance-Dragon-K609A-G00-13-0-NaturallySpeaking-Premium/dp/B00LX4BYV6

Scrivener

- https://www.literatureandlatte.com/store/scrivener?tab=Windows

Scrivener is advertised as Word processing software for fiction and screenplays. A few books I reviewed included this as an option that some writers are using. That is a very subjective opinion at best. I own a copy that I purchased a few years ago to use when writing my first book (after reading a book that recommended it). Scrivener is heavily suited for screen playwriting. I track word count to know if I want to include more research and expand the content. This is also important to determine the right size for the spine in the book cover. To see the word count, you have to export or compile the manuscript, which takes time. You will find this product better suited for a MAC over PC and for screenplays rather than writing a book.

Free website hosting
- https://wordpress.com/
- https://www.weebly.com/
- https://www.wix.com/

ABOUT THE AUTHOR

Richard Lang has published six books starting with the first book in 2012. The first book published was by purchasing the publishing rights of an original manuscript. Then rewrote the content to personalize the material.   The second and all other books were original content. Exploring different techniques to build a process for writing books. Books have ranged from business marketing and sales to self-help and project-related books. To goal of this book was to detail the different ways to not just write but the logistics to publishing a book. Also to dispel the myth, you can publish a book without doing much work. A good quality book requires research.